Great Artists

Diego Rivera

Joanne Mattern

ABDO
Publishing Company

visit us at
www.abdopub.com

Published by ABDO Publishing Company, 4940 Viking Drive, Edina, Minnesota 55435.
Copyright © 2005 by Abdo Consulting Group, Inc. International copyrights reserved in all
countries. No part of this book may be reproduced in any form without written permission from
the publisher. The Checkerboard Library™ is a trademark and logo of ABDO Publishing
Company.

Printed in the United States.

Cover Photo: Corbis
Interior Photos: Art Resource pp. 13, 17, 19, 21, 23, 27; Bridgeman Art Library p. 25; Corbis pp.
    1, 5, 9, 11, 29; Getty Images pp. 15, 18

Series Coordinator: Megan Murphy
Editors: Heidi M. Dahmes, Megan M. Gunderson
Cover Design: Neil Klinepier
Interior Design: Dave Bullen

Library of Congress Cataloging-in-Publication Data

Mattern, Joanne, 1963-
    Diego Rivera / Joanne Mattern.
      p. cm. -- (Great artists)
    Includes index.
    ISBN 1-59197-849-1
    1. Rivera, Diego, 1886-1957--Juvenile literature. 2. Painters--Mexico--Biography--Juvenile
literature. I. Title.

ND259.R5M34 2005
759.972--dc22
    [B]
                                                                    2004052811

Contents

Diego Rivera

Diego Rivera is a famous artist from Mexico. He painted many murals in Mexico and the United States. His style was different from anything people had seen before.

Rivera wanted to paint life the way it really was. He painted working people and individuals who lived simple lives. He also portrayed the different races of people who lived in Mexico. Rivera wanted his art to make others care more about the poor and uneducated.

Rivera often painted his political views. However, not everyone agreed with his opinions. So, many people got angry when they saw his works. But Rivera did not care. He kept painting the people and the scenes that were important to him.

Rivera showed everyday life in a dramatic new way. Today, Rivera is remembered as an artistic genius. Many people believe that he is the greatest Mexican painter of the twentieth century.

Rivera poured his excitement for life into his paintings.

Timeline

1886 ~ On December 8, José Diego María Rivera was born in Guanajuato, Mexico.

1894 ~ Rivera started school.

1902 ~ Rivera received a scholarship to continue his studies full-time at the Academy of San Carlos.

1906 ~ Rivera graduated from the academy.

1907 ~ Rivera began studying art in Madrid, Spain.

1913 to 1917 ~ Rivera created more than 200 Cubist paintings.

1923 ~ Rivera began painting murals on the Ministry of Education Building in Mexico City. His first one was titled *Creation*.

1926 to 1927 ~ Rivera painted frescoes in Chapingo, Mexico.

1932 ~ Rivera began painting murals for the Detroit Institute of Arts.

1933 ~ Rivera painted *Man at the Crossroads* for Rockefeller Center in New York.

1957 ~ On November 25, Rivera died of heart failure in Mexico City.

Fun Facts

- When he was older, Diego Rivera claimed that his full name was Diego María Conceptión Juan Nepomuceno Estanislao de la Rivera y Barrientos Acosta y Rodríguez.

- There are arguments over the exact date of Rivera's birth. His mother, an aunt, and a town hall document state that he was born on December 8. However, other records disagree and claim Rivera wasn't born until December 13.

- Rivera was not always a peaceful student. In 1903, he took part in a protest against the Academy of San Carlos's new director. The students were angry that the school did not teach Mexican art traditions. As a result of the protest, Rivera was suspended for more than two weeks.

José Diego María Rivera was born in Guanajuato, Mexico, on December 8, 1886. His parents were very happy when Diego and his twin brother, José Carlos, were born.

Diego's mother was María del Pilar Barrientos. She had already lost three babies before the twins were born. Sadly, Carlos died before he was two years old.

Diego's father was also named Diego Rivera. He owned a silver mine in Guanajuato. He was active in the local government. And, he worked as an author and a school inspector.

Diego was a curious little boy. He learned to read by age four. And, he liked to take toys apart to see how they worked. Drawing also interested young Diego.

Nothing in the house was safe from Diego's pencil. He covered the walls, doors, and furniture with his drawings. When Diego was four years old, his father set aside a room for him. He blanketed the walls with black cloth.

Now Diego could draw anything he wanted on the walls. Trains were one of his favorite things to draw. Diego spent hours at the train station in Guanajuato. Then, he drew pictures of all the things he had seen. He drew machines and battles, too.

Rivera's childhood home is now a museum.

Hard Times

In 1892, times were hard in Guanajuato. The silver mine that Diego's father invested in was unsuccessful. Soon, he was deeply in **debt**.

As a school inspector, Diego's father toured the countryside. He saw people suffering. And, he thought the government should do more to help them.

That year, Diego's mother decided to move the family. Diego's father was away on business at the time. But, his mother sold all the furniture and packed up Diego and his baby sister. The Riveras settled in Mexico City. Diego's father soon joined his family there. And, he got a job at the Department of Public Health.

Soon after the family moved, Diego got very sick. He could not go to school. Instead, he lay in bed drawing and reading. At this time, his aunt introduced him to Mexican **folk art**.

Guanajuato *is derived from a Native American word meaning "hill of frogs."*

School Days

After Diego got well, it was time to go to school. His family sent him to Catholic school in Mexico City in 1894. He lasted only three months there. He also quit the second school he attended. Diego did well at the third school. There, he skipped from third grade to sixth.

Diego still loved drawing soldiers and battle scenes. So, his father thought he should train for the army. Diego's father sent him to a military school called Colegio Militar. But, Diego was so unhappy that his parents took him out of the school.

At age nine, Diego began taking night courses at the Academy of San Carlos. Finally, he had found a school he liked. When he was only 11 years old, Diego began attending the academy full-time. In 1902, he won a **scholarship** to continue his studies there.

Diego did well at the academy. He studied under famous teachers. In 1905, Diego won a medal for painting. He exhibited 26 pieces of art at the final school show. Diego graduated from the Academy of San Carlos in 1906.

Rivera's years of drawing military scenes prepared him for this mural he later created for a building in Mexico City.

Traveling Artist

News of Rivera's talent as an artist spread quickly. After he graduated from the academy, he received a grant to study in Europe. The money was from Teodoro A. Dehesa, the governor of Veracruz, Mexico.

Rivera's **scholarship** did not start until January. So, he packed up his art supplies and left home. He wanted to learn more about Mexico. For a few months, Rivera traveled all over the country.

After exploring Mexico, Rivera was ready to begin his studies. He arrived in Madrid, Spain, in January 1907. He studied under a painter named Eduardo Chicharro y Aguera. Chicharro was influenced by **Impressionism** and Spanish **regionalism**.

Rivera studied under Chicharro for many years. But, Rivera developed his own style. While in Spain, Rivera sent paintings back home to Governor Dehesa. He needed to prove to Dehesa that he was working and deserved the scholarship.

When his **scholarship** ended, Rivera traveled throughout Europe. In each new city, Rivera copied works by other artists. He created his own works, too.

Rivera painted landscapes and ordinary people. He showed men working on the docks in Paris. He drew homeless people looking for food in the streets. Rivera worked long hours to become the best painter he could.

While traveling around Mexico, Rivera painted everything he saw. He even painted the highest mountain in Mexico, Pico de Orizaba, in Río Blanco.

Off to Paris

In 1910, Governor Dehesa permitted Rivera to return to Mexico. Dehesa wanted Rivera to exhibit his work at a show that celebrated Mexico's independence from Spain.

Rivera was happy to go home. But, he had fallen in love with a Russian artist named Angeline Beloff. They wanted to stay together, but Rivera had to return to Mexico. So, Beloff went home to Russia.

Back in Mexico, Rivera sold many paintings. Governor Dehesa's wife bought seven. And, she arranged for the government to purchase some of his other works. Rivera met many rich and powerful people at the art shows.

In May 1911, Rivera returned to Europe. Rivera and Beloff were reunited and happy to see each other again. They moved into a section of Paris that was filled with artists and writers. Rivera soon became friends with many artists, including Pablo Picasso, Georges Braque, and Piet Mondrian.

Cubism

The Cubist movement was a rejection of traditional painting methods. Cubism became very popular in the twentieth century. The style placed emphasis on flat surfaces, which was a new idea.

Shapes play an interesting role in Cubism. In these works, shapes are large, flat, and decorative. Cubist artists did not feel like they had to follow the rules about painting exactly what they saw. Instead, they focused on the structure of people and things. So, Cubist paintings seem to show many separate shapes which combine to form a larger object. This is seen in Rivera's Young Man with a Pen *(right).*

Color was an important element in Cubism, too. Color showed the relationship between the different elements in the painting. The colors added depth without distracting the viewer from the objects the artist wanted to represent.

While in Paris, Rivera learned about a style of art called Cubism. Between 1913 and 1917, he created more than 200 Cubist paintings. Then, he decided that Cubism was not realistic enough. Rivera still needed to find his own style of painting. He wanted to reach a wide audience with his ideas.

New Kind of Art

In 1914, **World War I** began in Europe. For the next four years, life in Paris was very hard. Millions of young men went off to fight on the battlefields. It was hard to find food in the city.

In 1916, Beloff gave birth to a son named Diego Jr. Beloff and Rivera loved their little boy. But, the baby was weak and became sick. There was not enough money for medicines or doctors. And, the apartment was cold because of a coal shortage. When he was about 14 months old, the little boy died.

Rivera was unhappy with his life and with Cubism. And, he had a falling-out with Picasso. So, Rivera decided to travel to Italy. There, he learned how to paint **frescoes** and murals. Rivera was

Rivera created this self-portrait for the cover of Time.

This sketch was for the Mexico mural project.

excited about these large, dramatic paintings. They could show so many exciting scenes!

Rivera thought about returning to Mexico to practice his new methods. He wanted to create art on Mexican buildings. This art would show the true story of the nation's history. In 1921, Rivera left Beloff and moved back home.

Back Home

Back in Mexico, Rivera met a woman named Guadalupe Marin. In 1922, Rivera and Marin were married. They later had two daughters, Lupe and Ruth.

Around the time of his marriage, Rivera became active in politics. He joined the **Communist** Party. Rivera had learned about communism while in Europe. He thought communism would help Mexico's poor people. Soon, his work reflected his beliefs.

The Mexican government and minister of education José Vasconcelos hired Rivera to paint murals on public buildings in Mexico. These paintings were very large, so everyone could see them. Even people who could not read understood the stories Rivera told with his murals.

In 1923, Rivera began painting the murals on the Ministry of Education Building in Mexico City. His first was titled *Creation*.

Creation

Rivera was not paid a lot of money for his paintings. He received about two dollars per 11 square feet (1 sq m). That was about the same pay an ordinary housepainter received.

Creation was painted on a wall of almost 1,000 square feet (93 sq m). Figures in the mural were more than 12 feet (4 m) tall. This can be seen in Primal Energy and Emergent Man *(right) from the center section of* Creation.

Several different artists were hired to work on the government's mural project. Unfortunately, many of their murals were **vandalized** in 1923 and 1924. Some artists were afraid for their safety at work and carried pistols. The government stopped supporting the artists in 1924.

Murals

In spite of all the trouble, Rivera kept painting. From 1926 to 1927, he also painted a former chapel at what is now the National School of Agriculture in Chapingo, Mexico. *Blood of the Revolutionary Martyrs Fertilizing the Earth* shows his use of bold colors.

In 1930, Rivera completed his work at the Ministry of Education. The 128 panels covered the stairways and walls of the building. The murals became famous around the world.

These paintings showed the everyday life of the Mexican people. Rivera became the leader of a new art movement. He brought **fresco** back into popularity.

But, not everyone in Mexico liked the mural project or Rivera's contributions to it. Many newspapers criticized the project. And, they condemned Rivera for how he depicted people.

Artist's Corner

Rivera's frescoes had their own distinct style. Rivera painted the Mexican peasants who lived hard, poor lives. He got the ideas for these images from his countrywide travels. He portrayed Mexican agriculture, industry, and customs.

With some of his murals, Rivera was criticized for making people that looked like monkeys. He emphasized his figures with strong outlines. He didn't spend much time on internal structures such as muscles and facial expressions. Instead, Rivera created simple figures and gave them life with bold colors.

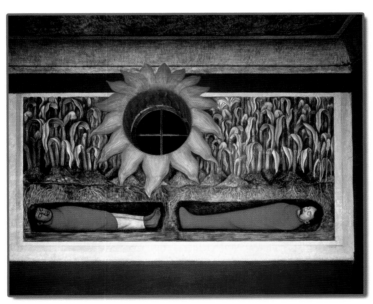

**Blood of the Revolutionary
Martyrs Fertilizing the Earth**

U.S. Projects

In 1927, Rivera and Marin had divorced. Around the same time, Rivera met a young artist named Frida Kahlo. Rivera loved Kahlo's fiery spirit and independence. On August 29, 1929, Rivera and Kahlo were married.

In 1930, Rivera and Kahlo went to the United States. At this time, Rivera was becoming famous there. Because of his popularity, Rivera was invited to paint a mural at the San Francisco Stock Exchange.

Rivera's mural was called *Allegory of California*. The painting shows a woman as a symbol of California. In her hands, she holds people working in the state's many different industries.

Starting in 1932, Rivera created murals for the Detroit Institute of Arts. The murals show the story of Detroit's industries. Rivera spent months filling the walls with factory scenes.

Rivera's **communist** beliefs were portrayed in the paintings. So, many people thought the **frescoes** were anti-American. But the institute defended him. Rivera felt it was some of his best work.

Production and Manufacture of Engine and Transmission *is the main panel on the north wall of the Detroit Institute mural.*

Production of Automobile Exterior and Final Assembly *is the main panel on the south wall of the Detroit Institute mural.*

Trouble

More trouble was waiting for Rivera in New York. In 1933, he painted a mural at Rockefeller Center in New York City. It was called *Man at the Crossroads*.

The **fresco** showed Rivera's hope for the future. However, one of the figures in the painting was not from the original approved plan. It was of Vladimir Lenin. In 1917, Lenin had created a new **communist** government in the Soviet Union.

At that time, Rockefeller Center was one of the new symbols of **capitalism**. Communists and capitalists had very different economic and political viewpoints. So, the mural's sponsors were not happy. In fact, Nelson Rockefeller wrote Rivera a letter asking him to replace Lenin's face.

Protests broke out. Newspapers and public meetings were filled with arguments about Rivera's work. But, Rivera thought his work would be accepted, as it was in Detroit.

In 1934, Rivera repainted Man at the Crossroads *in Mexico City. This detail is from the Mexican mural.*

Rivera believed that he would win the argument. He was wrong. Rivera's Rockefeller Center mural was destroyed. Later, Rivera repainted it at the Palace of Fine Arts in Mexico City.

Later Years

Rivera and Kahlo sailed home to Mexico in 1933. Rivera painted many more murals during the 1930s. His paintings were filled with the bright colors of Mexico. He celebrated his country's history and **culture** in his work.

Over the years, Rivera had collected many objects from Mexico's ancient culture. Finally, the collection grew so large that it needed a museum. So, Rivera built a building called Anahuacalli to hold the collection.

Frida Kahlo died on July 13, 1954. Rivera kept working and painting. In 1955, he married Emma Hurtado, who had been working as his art dealer. In September 1957, Rivera had a stroke. He tried to keep painting. But on November 25, 1957, Diego Rivera died of heart failure at his home in Mexico City.

The Mexican government decided Rivera should be buried in a place of honor in Mexico City. He was buried at the Rotunda of Illustrious Men in the Pantéon Dolores. Today, Rivera's murals continue to show us how paintings can change the world.

Diego Rivera and Frida Kahlo inspired each other to create beautiful art.

Glossary

capitalism - an economic system where businesses compete to sell their products and services.

communism - a social and economic system in which everything is owned by the government and given to the people as needed.

culture - the customs, arts, and tools of a nation or people at a certain time.

debt - something owed to someone, usually money.

folk art - art made by people with no formal training. It usually shows scenes from everyday life.

fresco - the art of painting on a wet surface that becomes hard when dry, such as a plaster wall.

Impressionism - an art movement developed by French painters in the late 1800s. They depicted the natural appearances of objects by using strokes or dabs of primary colors.

regionalism - emphasis on a geographic area and its characteristics.

scholarship - a gift of money to help a student pay for instruction.

vandalize - to intentionally damage public or private property.

World War I - from 1914 to 1918, fought in Europe. Great Britain, France, Russia, the United States, and their allies were on one side. Germany, Austria-Hungary, and their allies were on the other side.

Saying It

Guanajuato - gwah-nah-HWAH-toh
José Diego María Rivera - hoh-SAY DYAY-goh mah-REE-ah ree-BAY-ray
Vladimir Lenin - VLAD-uh-mihr LEHN-uhn

Web Sites

To learn more about Diego Rivera, visit ABDO Publishing Company on the World Wide Web at **www.abdopub.com**. Web sites about Rivera are featured on our Book Links page. These links are routinely monitored and updated to provide the most current information available.

Index